EVENING MANTRAS

EVENING MANTRAS

FOR A PEACEFUL NOW
AND AN INSPIRING TOMORROW

CICO BOOKS
LONDON NEW YORK

Published in 2017 by CICO Books
An imprint of Ryland Peters & Small Ltd
20–21 Jockey's Fields   341 E 116th St
London WC1R 4BW   New York, NY 10029

www.rylandpeters.com

10 9 8 7 6 5 4 3 2 1

Design © CICO Books 2017

For photography credits, see pages 143–144.

A CIP catalog record for this book is available from
the Library of Congress and the British Library.

ISBN: 978-1-78249-539-0

Printed in China

Commissioning editor: Kristine Pidkameny
Senior editor: Carmel Edmonds
Designer: Paul Tilby
Art director: Sally Powell
Production manager: Gordana Simakovic
Publishing manager: Penny Craig
Publisher: Cindy Richards

INTRODUCTION

Ending your day well will lead to a better night's sleep and a more productive tomorrow. Within this book you will find a collection of carefully selected words, mantras, and quotations that will inspire you to reflect, appreciate, and dream.

Beautifully presented, every mantra will empower you to bring your day to a calm close ready for the next. Some mantras are helpful reminders to take the time to relax so you feel restored from the day's activities. Others encourage you to wonder more and worry less. The words of wisdom here guide you to nurture and find balance in your relationships, not only with family and friends, but also with yourself.

You can use these mantras in a number of ways. You may wish to read one every night, perhaps at the start of the evening when you need a new perspective, or right before going to bed so the thought stays with you while you sleep. Try writing down your favorites in a journal, or on cards to keep on a nightstand or maybe to put under your pillow. You could even send them to friends or family for inspiration.

SEE THE EVENING AS IF FOR THE FIRST TIME...

You'll discover the gifts of gratitude, delight, and being present.

THERE
IS
ALWAYS
SOMETHING
TO
BE
GRATEFUL
FOR

BE TRUTHFUL, GENTLE,
AND FEARLESS

ALL SHALL BE WELL,
AND ALL SHALL BE WELL,
AND ALL MANNER OF THINGS
SHALL BE WELL.

Julian of Norwich

WHAT WE THINK, WE BECOME

Buddha

I KNOW NOTHING
WITH ANY CERTAINTY,
BUT THE SIGHT OF STARS
MAKES ME DREAM.

Vincent van Gogh

BE THE SPARK ESPECIALLY WHEN IT'S DARK

IF THE ONLY PRAYER YOU
EVER SAY IN YOUR ENTIRE LIFE
IS THANK YOU,
IT WILL BE ENOUGH.

Meister Eckhart

TAKE REST:

A FIELD THAT HAS RESTED GIVES
A BEAUTIFUL CROP.

Ovid

PUT YOUR THOUGHTS TO SLEEP,
DO NOT LET THEM CAST A SHADOW
OVER THE MOON OF YOUR HEART.
LET GO OF THINKING.

Rumi

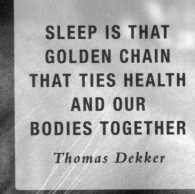

SLEEP IS THAT GOLDEN CHAIN THAT TIES HEALTH AND OUR BODIES TOGETHER

Thomas Dekker

CONNECT WITH YOUR DIVINE SOURCE

GOOD
THINGS
TAKE
TIME

WE DO NOT LEARN FROM EXPERIENCE...
WE LEARN FROM REFLECTING ON EXPERIENCE

UNPLUG

WORRYING WILL NEVER
CHANGE THE OUTCOME.

LET IT GO.

A CERTAIN DARKNESS IS NEEDED TO SEE THE STARS.

ONCE YOU MAKE A DECISION,
THE UNIVERSE CONSPIRES
TO MAKE IT HAPPEN.

Ralph Waldo Emerson

WELCOME THE BEGINNING OF A NEW EVENING

DELIGHT AT THE PROMISE
OF A NEW TOMORROW

VERY LITTLE
IS NEEDED
TO MAKE A
HAPPY LIFE;
IT IS ALL
WITHIN
YOURSELF,
IN YOUR
WAY OF
THINKING

Marcus Aurelius

NEVER
STOP
LOOKING
UP

TRUST IN DREAMS,
FOR IN THEM
IS HIDDEN
THE GATE TO ETERNITY

Kahlil Gibran

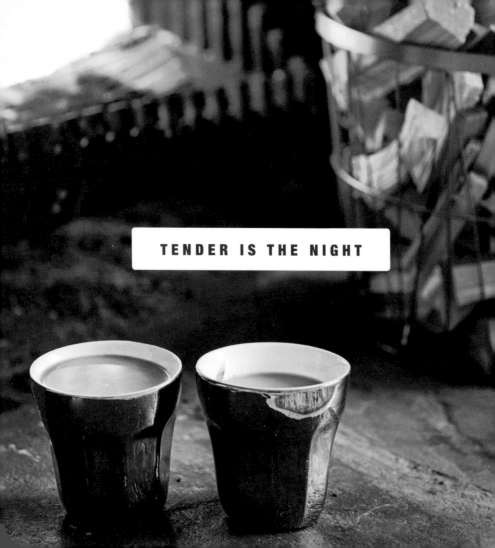

TENDER IS THE NIGHT

HITCH YOUR WAGON
TO A STAR

Ralph Waldo Emerson

If a little dreaming is dangerous, the cure for it is not to dream less but to dream more, to dream all the time.

Marcel Proust

WHAT YOU SEEK
IS SEEKING YOU

Rumi

RIGHT TIME, RIGHT PLACE;
ASTONISH YOURSELF TONIGHT

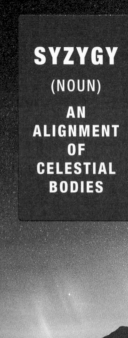

SYZYGY

(NOUN)

AN ALIGNMENT OF CELESTIAL BODIES

EMBRACE THE POWER
OF THE EVENING SKY

RELAX AS IT IS

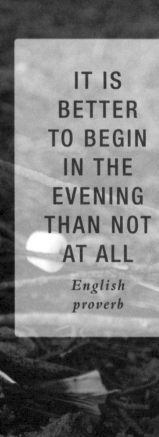

IT IS
BETTER
TO BEGIN
IN THE
EVENING
THAN NOT
AT ALL

*English
proverb*

TONIGHT, CHOOSE EASE

**TO THE MIND THAT IS STILL,
THE WHOLE UNIVERSE SURRENDERS**

Lao Tzu

LIVE IN
TRUTH
AND THE
TRUTH
WILL
PROTECT
YOU

ANTICIPATE THE DIFFICULT BY MANAGING THE EASY

Lao Tzu

**EVEN THE LONGEST DAY
HAS ITS END**

Irish proverb

DON'T
WAIT.
THE
TIME
WILL
NEVER
BE
JUST
RIGHT.

*Mark
Twain*

Thousands of candles can be lighted from a single candle, and the life of the candle will not be shortened. Happiness never decreases by being shared.

Buddha

A BEAUTIFUL SUNSET THAT WAS
MISTAKEN FOR A DAWN

Claude Debussy

AT CLOSE OF DAY
I FIND MY
PLACE OF EASE

THE ONLY
MIRACLES
THAT CAN'T REACH YOU
ARE THE ONES
YOU WAIT
AROUND FOR

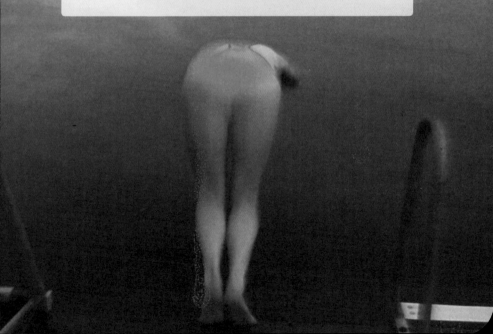

THERE REALLY IS
NO BETTER TIME THAN NOW

Sir Walter Scott

COURAGE IS FEAR
THAT HAS SAID ITS PRAYERS

MY SUN SETS TO RISE AGAIN

Robert Browning

Silence

is a source

of great

strength

Lao Tzu

LISTEN WITH YOUR HEART

THERE'S NO BETTER SOUND TO HEAR
THAN THE OCEAN, THE WIND, AND THE RAIN
ALL AT ONCE, LATE AT NIGHT

THERE IS A TIME
FOR MANY WORDS,
AND THERE IS ALSO
A TIME FOR SLEEP

Homer

LET TOMORROW
BE TOMORROW

WHAT LIES BEHIND YOU AND
WHAT LIES IN FRONT OF YOU
PALES IN COMPARISON TO WHAT
LIES INSIDE OF YOU.

Ralph Waldo Emerson

CHOOSE LOVE OVER FEAR—EVERY TIME

STARS CAN'T
SHINE WITHOUT
DARKNESS

FROM REALLY FAR
OUT IN SPACE
DO YOU KNOW WHAT
YOU LOOK LIKE?
A SUPER STAR

IT DOES NOT
REQUIRE MANY WORDS
TO SPEAK
THE TRUTH

Chief Joseph

HONOR THE STILLNESS

A LOVING
HEART
IS THE
TRUEST
WISDOM

*Charles
Dickens*

LET THE BEAUTY OF WHAT YOU LOVE
BE WHAT YOU DO

Rumi

YOU DON'T HAVE TO REACH FOR THE STARS, THEY ARE ALREADY WITHIN YOU

**MUSIC IN
THE SOUL
CAN BE
HEARD BY
THE UNIVERSE**

Lao Tzu

RELAX TO THE SOUND OF
THE GENTLE EVENING RAIN

THE SIMPLE JOYS
ARE THE GREAT ONES

WRITE IT ON YOUR HEART THAT EVERY DAY
IS THE BEST DAY IN THE YEAR

Ralph Waldo Emerson

TRUST

IN THE

PRESENT

MOMENT

No act of kindness,
no matter how small,
is ever wasted

Aesop

GREAT ACTS
ARE MADE UP OF
SMALL DEEDS

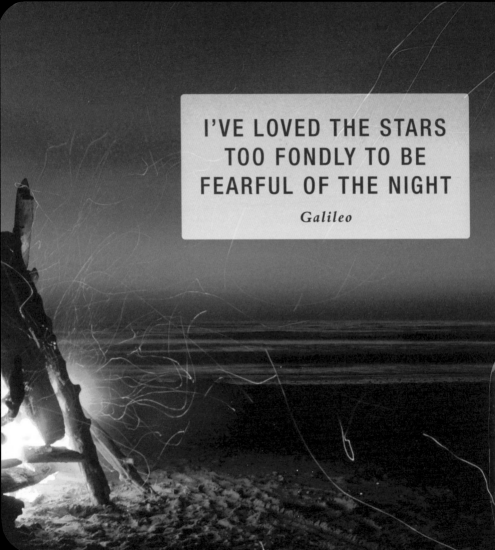

I'VE LOVED THE STARS
TOO FONDLY TO BE
FEARFUL OF THE NIGHT

Galileo

MY GUIDING WORD IS SERENITY

GOOD NIGHT,
SWEET DREAMS

MAY THE FIREFLIES ON A SUMMER'S
EVE LIGHT UP YOUR PATH

AND REMEMBER, NO MATTER WHERE YOU GO, THERE YOU ARE

Confucius

DREAMS DO COME TRUE

**BUILD UPON TODAY
A BRIDGE TO THE FUTURE**

TOMORROW AWAITS

DO LESS

LIVE MORE

THE BEST PREPARATION FOR TOMORROW IS TO DO TODAY'S WORK SUPERBLY WELL

William Osler

SHOW UP AND EMBRACE POSSIBILITY

SLEEPING TO DREAM

IT IS ONLY THROUGH SHADOWS
THAT ONE COMES TO KNOW THE LIGHT

Saint Catherine of Siena

SEE TOMORROW WITH FRESH EYES

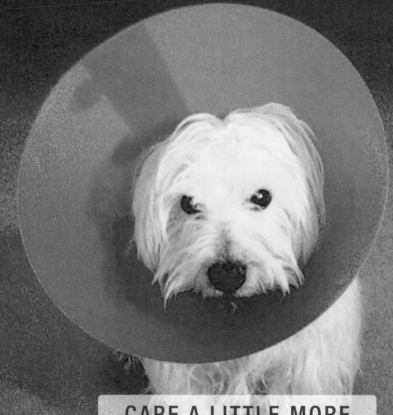

CARE A LITTLE MORE

IMAGINE THE POSSIBILITIES

SLEEP
DREAM
BELIEVE

EVEN IF I KNEW THAT TOMORROW THE WORLD WOULD GO TO PIECES, I WOULD STILL PLANT MY APPLE TREE.

Martin Luther

INSPIRE HOPE

ALL THE FLOWERS
OF ALL THE TOMORROWS
ARE IN THE
SEEDS OF TODAY

Indian proverb

THE FUTURE IS NO MORE UNCERTAIN THAN THE PRESENT

Walt Whitman

WE CONVINCE BY OUR PRESENCE

Walt Whitman

SHARE A CUP OF KINDNESS

BE HAPPY
FOR NO REASON

BECAUSE
YOU CAN

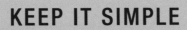
KEEP IT SIMPLE

**NATURE DOES NOT HURRY,
YET EVERYTHING IS ACCOMPLISHED**

Lao Tzu

OH, THE SUMMER NIGHT,
HAS A SMILE OF LIGHT,
AND SHE SITS ON
A SAPPHIRE THRONE

Byron Procter

THE STARS ARE
THE STREET LIGHTS
OF ETERNITY

KNOWLEDGE COMES, BUT WISDOM LINGERS

Alfred, Lord Tennyson

THE JOURNEY IS THE REWARD

Taoist proverb

NO

SNOWFLAKE

EVER

FALLS

IN

THE

WRONG

PLACE

Zen proverb

WONDER IS THE BEGINNING
OF WISDOM

Ancient proverb

START WHERE YOU ARE

DOWNTIME IS YOUR TIME

COLOR OUTSIDE THE LINES

FOLLOW YOUR JOY

MEET
YOUR
TRUE
SELF

TO ALL, TO EACH, A FAIR GOOD NIGHT,
AND PLEASING DREAMS, AND
SLUMBERS LIGHT

Sir Walter Scott

THE SETTING SUN OFFERS AN
INVITATION TO WONDER

THE GREATEST MIRACLE OF ALL IS FOUND IN WHAT IS MOST ORDINARY

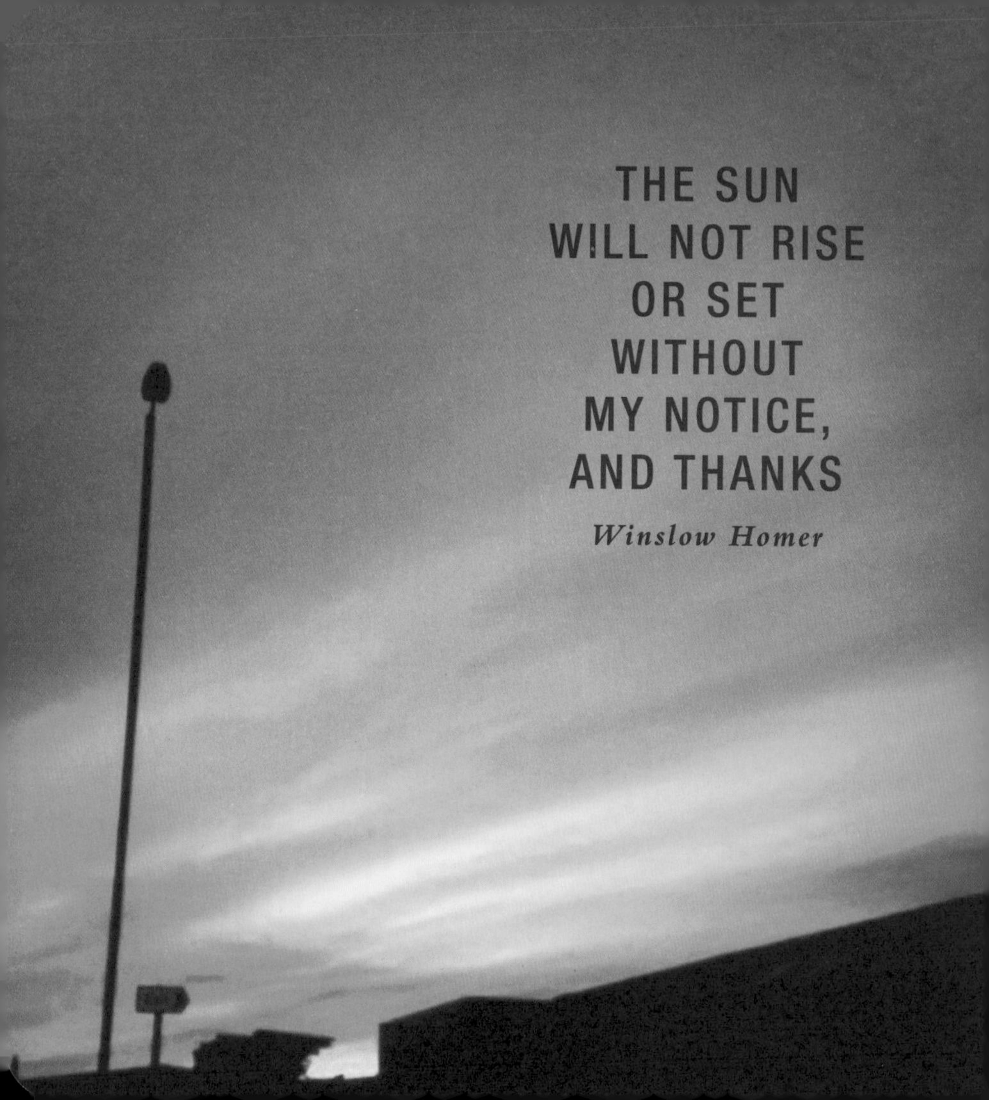

THE SUN
WILL NOT RISE
OR SET
WITHOUT
MY NOTICE,
AND THANKS

Winslow Homer

THERE IS GUIDANCE
FOR EACH OF US, AND
BY LOVELY LISTENING,
WE SHALL HEAR
THE RIGHT WORD

Ralph Waldo Emerson

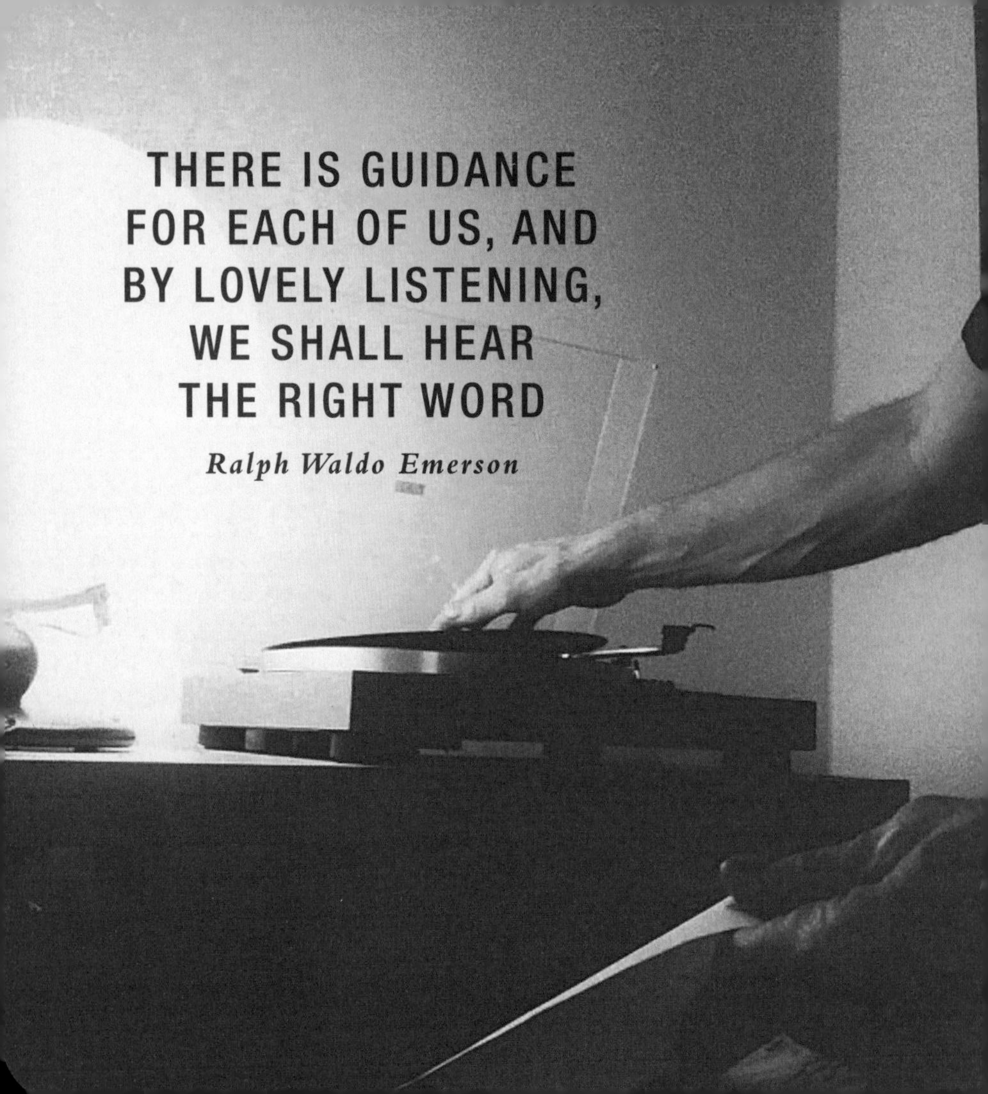

THE
WISDOM
YOU
SEEK
IS
ALWAYS
IN
YOUR
HEART

YOU HAVE NOT LIVED TODAY UNTIL YOU
HAVE DONE SOMETHING FOR SOMEONE
WHO CAN NEVER REPAY YOU

John Bunyan

THREE THINGS
CANNOT BE
LONG HIDDEN:
THE SUN,
THE MOON,
AND
THE TRUTH

Buddha

SMALL
GESTURES
MAKE
A BIG
DIFFERENCE

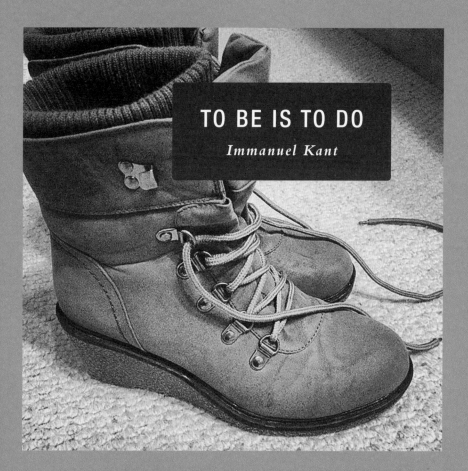

TO BE IS TO DO

Immanuel Kant

HAPPINESS DEPENDS
UPON OURSELVES

Aristotle

IT'S NOT WHAT HAPPENS TO YOU, BUT HOW YOU REACT TO IT THAT MATTERS

Epictetus

I AM
AT HOME
IN THE
WORLD

PICTURE CREDITS